Soulful

The Great Escape

A little chapbook by Jenny Berry

Spoiler alert: *I didn't think of my own title, but I promise I wrote everything else. The title was the name given to my workshops in one particular prison. Apparently, poetry helps you to escape…*

A MESSAGE FROM THE AUTHOR

Hello, I'm Jen…

I identify as an apostrophe because I'm small, up in the air, everyone gets me wrong and, at times, I'm possessive. I'm a lover of words (the whole spectrum of words) and I guess I believe the 'pen *really* is mightier than the sword'.

I regularly express myself through written poetry, spoken word performances, podcast, radio hosting and more recently script writing.

This little chapbook is based on my experiences of delivering workshops and performing poetry in prisons. As with every great story it started something like this:

"Once upon a time in the North West of England a poet cold-called a local prison and boldly asked if she could volunteer to host workshops and perform some poetry…"

That's it. It's a short story. A short story with no sign of ending because the narrative keeps exploring real life characters. Basically, the prison said 'yes' and before I knew it, I was regularly helping prisoners to express themselves from behind the confines of the prison walls.

This volunteering opportunity allowed me to form so many new connections, both inside and outside of the prison system and despite not earning anything from my time, I felt abundant each time I left the prison knowing that in small way I was able to bring art and creativity to people from all walks of life. I was able to see 'people' not just 'prisoners'.

Then, in 2015, I was encouraged by Dr. Martin Henery from the University of Manchester, Masood Entrepreneurship Centre to enter a competition and I won £10k to set up a social enterprise CIC to help me broaden my work.

That was just the sign I needed from the universe to firmly anchor myself in the messy business of serving others combining passion, poetry and real people. That's exactly what I have been doing since then…

The prelude to the story goes something like this…

I was a ridiculously shy girl and without knowing how, I became an enormously cocky young woman. Poetry was my antidote to the harsh world I found myself in and I've certainly experienced my own form of imprisonment with Body Dysmorphia. This condition trained me in the fine art of not judging others too quickly and my cockiness evolved into compassion.

This book is not just about my poetry - there are other artists involved. Four different prisoners contributed their artwork for this book and a photographer took 3 photos. This collaborative ethos is something that I feel is deeply necessary to improve society. *No man is an island* – not even those behind 4 walls.

Jenny Berry
www.jennyberry.co.uk

CHAPTERS

BANGED UP [1]

It's all about perspective

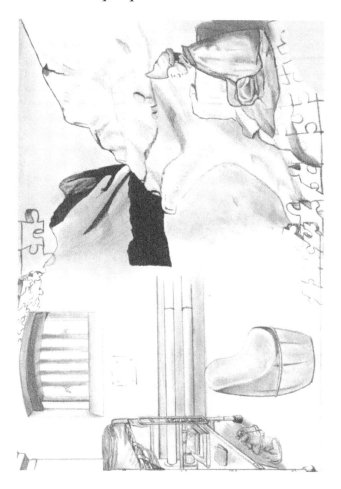

BUTTERFLY THINKING
Daydreaming can get you through the day

Casually checking her own fingernails
Chomped cuticles are dismissed
Cracked knuckles expose narratives untold
That which present-day fake-tan attempts to cover

A lifetime of unnourished moments
Can be detected in her expression
Yet her features remain chiseled
Framing the catastrophic historical mishaps
And fuck ups of her existence

She's still beautiful

Her yellow tinged eyes
And cig-stained teeth
Yell a thousand stories silently
Her boldest feature is her smile and it's flaunted

This bitch is banged up, but her thoughts are her own
Therefore, she's free

A HAIKU IN YOUR HEAD
Emancipation is all in the mind

Strong minded inmates

Are footloose and fancy free

It's all an outlook

DENIAL
Different jail, same face, broken people all around

Occasionally their words echoed on
Longer than their sentences

One cell door slammed, another opened
Mirroring sentiments reflected onto the wing

"I'm changing this time for good"

Some did, many tried, a few gave up the last time they
checked in

Certain families made it impossible, snorting off the cards
they'd been dealt and chipping away at each other's shoulders

Some miracles happened, lighting up the wings like the
Hacienda Nightclub at its peak

A select few were polite enough to wish me well and said that
they looked forward to seeing me again soon

HOW LONG YOU GOT?
Some accept their sentences, others do not

How long mate?
How long's a piece of string?

Hanging around your neck, pre-suicide position
Clinging onto depression's ammunition
To tip toe you to the other side
The other side of life, which is death
Or a different way of thinking
Instead of selling drugs and winking at the
bad boy way of living the dream

Some embrace the time
Prefer the grime
For a bit of time off
From real life
A vacation from a real wife
And two point four kids
Avoiding
Public houses serving addiction
Lifetime subscriptions to
Maybe's
And might's

For some, time ticks on post prison
Living a sentence in their head
A lifelong self-punishment to the soul
Wishing for dead

Others shake the mistakes
Clutching family and mates

Don't ask me how long you've got
Because its measure's down to fate
It differs for all...mate

ALL IN A DAY'S WORK [2]
The world can turn upside down in one shift

ANGEL WINGS
Many prison staff literally eat, live and breathe recovery

This place
Is known for its waste of space
He's off his case
It's the commonplace
For those marginalized dropouts

Overlooked by those tucked in a book
Not giving a fuck
Re-reading the statistics
Not the truth

The indigenous digits record real time
Breakfast times
Burnt toast on the wing times
More than the petty crimes

The grown-ups that can't read
With pockets full of shame
Interpreted the same
As being thick

Hidden, dyslexic, anorexic
Tongue tied taboos
Written off
With cigs and booze

And limited beliefs

No-one hears the good stuff
Sensationalism sells
Well so do chips
And I'm keeping it real, man

Like all those that rose

After misdiagnosed
Conditions were
Corrected

Staff pushing pride
Not grades
Making sure the stuff inside
Doesn't fade

Because it's you - only you that can change
There are young dads dancing behind bars
Rubbing the Reebok classics together three times
Because there's no place like home

There's no place like home
When you're no longer a dickhead
When you have a place in your family's embrace
Because you've changed

Press prints of the drug trenched raids
Corrupt staff and hidden blades
Let's call a spade a spade
It's no laugh
Complexities from way back yonder
There's no magic wand
No spell book to ponder
There are angels

Angels in fancy dress as prison guards
And listeners, mentors, teachers
Carrying whispers of hope
And light
Emerging in the darkness
Reincarnating life
In those who have died inside
They're the angels of our wings

FIFTY / FIFTY
You never know what is going on in someone's head

Hope perches itself between the prison cracks

Making an appearance in those short private moments

It pauses on bristles of toothbrushes

Curls up inside empty toilet roll holders and clings to the
inside stitching of prison pillows

Belief is everywhere if you squint hard enough

Beneath the grit you can feel love in its own experienced form

For some, love bounces in the door, clasped onto a shirt cuff
fresh from court

Odours of hope and confidence, freshly bottled from the out
remain on its collar

Some carry traces of love in their tear ducts, like dried up lakes
begging for rain, they crave visits like a baby needs milk

Optimism flutters across wings, depending on what kind of
day it has been

It could go either way

DRAGON FIRE
Old habits die hard

They tip-toed around his circles of fire
Half scared, half bored of the incessant burns
Whiplash propelled from his tongue
His own saliva bathed in acid to cool down

The black hole inhabited his left eye
His right eye wore scars like a Rolex
His volcanic temperament
Made him famous

The other residents shared revulsion and fear
The staff painted a nine to five smile
and dreaded each shift
The guy didn't give a shit

His nauseating persona stained the atmosphere
His crimes were like office gossip
Everyone had heard the stories
Only an inexperienced apprentice would dare ask

His scaly wings would burn as he passed through
His tail was once between his legs
But now thick, scaly and free
Leaving etched warning signs on the ground behind him

He relit his own fire with petrol
Provoking the flames inside
He knew he would commit again and not abstain
And, so did everyone else

SUPERHEROES
Imagine hating hair and then going to be a hairdresser

Did you know Paul's being released?
He came on my course
He attended mine too
I trained him in the gym, me
I made him brand new

I think I was his inspiration
I think I empowered
It was my dedication
He thinks I'm high powered

Yeah, mate, I helped him too
He was on my wing
I was his screw
Recovery's just my thing

He was a closed book
Yet he opened up to me
I gave his courage a pluck
I helped him you see

I was his saviour
And tomorrow's my one to one
He'll do my career a favour
Then another scumbag gone

DOMINO EFFECT [3]

HYSTERICS
Sometimes in life, you need to laugh, or you'll literally cry

We used to holiday twice a year
Drinking champagne on ice
We'd wear matching gym gear
Share naan bread and lemon rice

We had sex in every position
Fifty shades of knackered
An all-night competition
My favorite flowers scattered

Now we have a phone card
Igniting our sexy time
Echoes from the prison guards
And a dodgy prison line

You talk of your cell mate snoring
Along with his bad breath
You're not happy with the flooring
And you're clearly bored to death

Our relations have somewhat changed
We've an overbearing drought
But babe it feels too strange
So, just call me when you're out

EMPTY HOUSE
Every action has a reaction

She doesn't want to go to an empty house
With the only light from the curtains crack
And the tap dripping to the beat of
Silence

She doesn't want to go to an empty house
Where unused cups sit beside uneaten bagels
And tea towels remain un-creased
Where eggs stay unbroken and
The bread is deceased
You see, she wants the splash of the tap
Filling the cup, bites into the bagel
Caffeine driven conversation
And she wants to just watch

She doesn't care about the chats
Context
Or facts
She wants to sit back
Be the audience for a while
Sinking into the synchronisation of sounds

She doesn't want to go to an empty house
She enjoys the echoes of others
Woes and worries they uncover
She leisurely listens to their laughter
Because always, always, after
Her house is empty but her mind's full

I THINK
Through the eyes of a child

Me mam's in the big house
I think it's dead posh

Me mam's doing bird
I think she's gonna be a vet

Me mam's in the slammer
I think she's doing battle raps

Me mam's in a cell
I think it's like a cellar

Me mam went off the rails
I think she was on a train

Me mam's doing time
I think she's learning about clocks

Me mam's doing a stretch
I think she's learning yoga

Me mam's being taught a lesson
I think she's being a teacher

Me mam's got given a cat c
I think she prefers dogs

Me mam's living on a wing
I think she can fly

Me mam's at work
I think

TO WHOMEVER YOU WISH THIS RANT
Sometimes a rant is all we need

Like a battered empty petrol tank
You're going nowhere quick
A societal odd-ball skank
You personify sick

Like a cheap stolen tyre
You're punctured, damaged goods
Disgustingly dire
Your truth's as clear as mud

Like a dented cig-dimped dashboard
You're next to be replaced
Arrogantly self-assured
You were born a bad taste

Like a corroded wedged-shut sunroof
You stake away the light
Taking everything and more
You marinate your words in shite

Like a clapped-out gear stick
You're jammed in one drive
You knock society sick
No-one wants you alive

A CLASS ACT
People are people, with different circumstances

We've expected actions of people and classes
An indentation on society's masses
A mauled with, tainted, interpretation
Of postal code identification

  Working-class with its classical connotations
  Take a middle-class lass with binocular observations
  A sky-rise peep into the working man
  Misses the point. He's doing all he can

    Some shoulders are chipped
    And doused in bitter endings
    It's not fuckin' fair, no-one cares
    About us and lack of spending

  Sometimes the suited and booted
  Aren't always saluted
  And the council estate of mind
  Isn't just that kind

The postal code combination
Shouldn't carry contemplation
It's the person inside
Those families who reside
Those are all we should judge

HIGH RISK
No matter who we are, it's the small things in life

I'm high risk me miss

Ok I said

Yeah miss high risk

Did you hear ? I'm high risk me miss

High maintenance, you mean?

Nar mate

Prison mask dissolved

Boyish banter weakened

Little boy poised inside adult body

With facial hair piercing surface of chin

No wisdom yet birthed

High fucking maintenance, he said

Little boyish tantrum

Nourished with nicotine-stained memories

And spiced up narcotic notions

Erupted rapidly in the classroom

He'd found himself lost

Lost for an opponent of his words

Miss, I miss being missed - no-one misses me no more

What do you miss the most ? I asked

Sex with the wife and a curry

SHIT STICKS
The papers say it's an easy ride

The floors are stained in self-pity
uncertainty lingers
Guilt trips fly high
Pirouetting with paranoia
Broken wings drop guilty feathers
Fluffing prison pillows with fear
Shit sticks when you're inside
Shit sticks our kid

Biscuit tin minds
Bouncing from cell walls
Trails of crumbs
Trying to find their way home
God it's hard, Miss
Stuck in a cycle
Etched on pattern
God its hard, Miss

The petty crimes
Take up too big a time
The shorter sentences
Don't work
They're scumbags
Taking taxpayers money
Living VIP with a cell TV
And it's all on me

Society's narrative echoes blindly
From pixels of half a picture painted
Families cut blade of shame
Leaving pop-up paper
family pictures framed
Criminal records on cv
Showcasing an ex-con

Vacant jobs shy away
Past applicants need not apply
Some housed in prison
Then do time on the streets
With a box for a bed
And a paper for sheets

Rotating round
The prison doors spin
The prison playground
Carries heads in bins
Hearts on sleeves
Hope on pins
With funding thieves
No-one wins

Broken wings drop guilty feathers
Fluffing prison pillows with fear
Shit sticks when you're inside
Shit sticks, our kid

CHANCERS
A very repetitive story

Dear anyone new on the wing who might listen

I'm not guilty

The end

INSIDE OUT [5]

HMP Manchester

MY EX IS AROUND THE CORNER
Sometimes, we are imprisoned by our thoughts

The annoying, exasperating existence
Like living bacteria from a distance
Or bed bugs under your cover
Of an irritating ex-lover

Like recurring meningitis
A bad migraine or cystitis
Or being struck by lightning twice
Seeing the ex is never nice

Peculiar and impetuous
Society is incestuous
It hinders, grates and vexes
When bumping into your exes

Haunting like a spirit
Or a lingering distasteful lyric
As you attempt with desperation
To avoid all conversation

Like an off-Sambuca
Or violent verruca
They were never here when needed
Now it's like they've been bleedin' breeded

Reminders on twitter
It really is a shitter
You'd have watched the Men in Black
Back-to-back

And then Shawshank Redemption
Before getting their attention
Like a fart in a lift
A smell you'd like to shift

Like antibiotics that won't work
Or a cough you can't shirk
Or conjunctivitis with no fear

Oh, how I wish my ex would FUCKING disappear

A GIRL LIKE ME
It's important to bring the outside in

They said...

Why go in prison, a girl like you?

Why shouldn't I? - I'd say...

I've seen it all mate –

Men in need of meds

Choking on mental health

Women carrying

Prison-grown placentas

Like contraband

Revealed on sticks

It takes the piss -

Crap from cell windows

Thrown to rats on shoes

Unnourished inmates

Starved of dignity

And staff -

I've seen guilty, misjudged and messed up

I've seen heads fall off

Hearts smashed on cell walls

I've seen miracles -

I've seen families re-unite

Grown-ups learn to read, flicking through pages of Pam Ayers

Pads of fingers feeling education, not smack

Miss, one said, *I should have looked after my teeth*

Laughter melted bars on windows

Inviting more prisoners in

Drug-dissolved teeth, yet no broken smile

I'll never forget him

Mothers aggression -

post-natal depression

Breast feeding behind bars

But mums still being mums

Chatter of stretch marks and big bums

I've witnessed staff save lives

By the tip of their tongue

Tiptoeing around the right words

To say...

I've seen Governors eat humble pie -

Wardens with an ego

Corrupt staff caught and sacked

And lies

Most of all -

I've seen communication

Mindsets changing through education

Prisoners will walk through the gate

Let the door shut, not rotate, mate

We can't afford it

The country is in a state

That's why I go in there

Yep, a girl like me

JAIL BIRD
Freedom comes in all shapes and sizes

I'm a jail bird me
A repeat offender
I've been banged up so much
I've surrendered
The wings take off from time to time
I cling to the feathers
Ruffed up from my mind

You may have heard
Of doing bird
But the stretch
Makes me wretch
And internally fetch
A bad cellmate
A mate not a friend
Not one to depend
And not one to offend
No offence

An unwanted squatter

Crouching on my thoughts
Telling me I ought
To be thinner
I'm not a winner
The structure of my face
Is an unfiltered disgrace
Without a filler

Filling my head with Cat B
Some days Cat D
Bolting my cell
Telling me I'm not free
To be me
Myself

I'm a jailbird
I know imprisonment inside out
I've climbed the walls
I've signed up to education
Argued legislation
Blamed our generation

For my sentence

The sentence in my head
With the sentiments I've said
Living licensed conditions
Embracing Suspicions
High fiving
Confidence lackin
Thought cracking
Self-talk

I'm a jailbird
But right now, I'm free

BABY OLYMPICS
A mum is a mum, no matter where they are

Are you sure? I did a test
A digital one, they're the best
They give a date
Are you sure you're preggers
And not just late?

How's your morning sickness?
Mine's a curse
How's yours?
Yeah, mine's worse
How are your boobs?
Mine are bigger

Can you face food?
How's your figure?
I'm still a size 8, me!
I'm hardly showing.
I'll have no stretch marks me,
The way it's going.

You exercising?
You avoiding pate?
I run and swim, me
Ain't touched a latte
What buggy you getting?
What birth you having?
Have you got a plan?

Which hospital you going?
Have you had a 20d scan?
You donating your stem cells?
You eating your placenta?
Do you have a doula?
I do, mine's cooler

What was labour like?
Were you too posh to push?
I did it natural me
No fuss!

Such a body needed stitches
Thingy was induced
Was it you with the epidural?
Or was it the ventose?
What name have you chosen?
What was the weight?
Were you on time?
Or past your date?

Do you breast feed?
Breast is best!
Are you calm?
I never panic, me
Carry a kid in each arm

How old's yours now?
Are they smiling?
Are they sleeping?
Can they sit up?
Are they rolling?
Are they pointing?
Are they using their hands?
Are they meeting their milestones?
Are you sure your's understands?

Mine does
Mines smiling
Crawling
Sleeping through
Has done since their first night
Mine sits up
Points and rolls

Smashing all their milestone goals

Is yours a good eater?
Is yours a good talker?
Mine's on solids
And an advanced walker

I did baby led, me
No spoon needed
Like breastfeeding
I succeeded

My kids are perfect
I find motherhood fun
Who the fuck am I kidding?
I'm a knackered
Competitive
Insecure mum

THANK YOU...

To Simon Bland from HMP Leicester for introducing me to my publisher Shobana Patel. Because of this stroke of destiny, I was able to partner with the beautiful Soulful Group who offered me the opportunity to publish my experiences of the prison system.

To my husband Nick, and the friends and family who constantly give me confidence to explore different worlds within my writing practice and to never give up.

To the photographer, Mick Steff who has provided the most exquisite photograph for the front cover and two other photographs for the book.

To Franklin, Eyeball, CM and A Resident from HMP Buckley Hall for the artwork to accompany my chapter headings. Every prisoner who submitted their artwork will be exhibited in The Arc outside Manchester Prison.

To Tina Patel, who helped me liaise internally with prison staff and prisoners to accomplish great things within my poetry sessions, some of which are displayed in this book.

To Dr. Martin Henery and everyone involved within the Masood Entrepreneurship Centre and the Venture Further competition.

To Graham Hartill for golden advice on writing for wellbeing and for a day shadowing him in his writer in residency role at Parc Prison.

To POPS Charity for commissioning me to work within different prisons alongside other activities their charity provides.

To TiPP Charity for commissioning me to work with both male and female prisoners performing and using poetry alongside the other activities they provide.

And most of all, to every single person who attended and attends future workshops inside and outside of prison. The one most inspired in every room is always me.

THE POWER OF ART & CREATIVITY IN PRISONS...

Art can be hugely important to people in custody. In an environment that controls and instructs how you conduct your day, how to behave, what you can eat, a place that removes you from those people and things that you love and enjoy, it can cause enormous stress and despair. Art in prison can offer you the opportunity to express yourself freely, to be creative, unrestrained and to have hope.

Rob Knight | Governor HMP Manchester

"I now know how to express myself without throwing my fists around"
A Prisoner from a North West Prison

"If this was in the community it would keep me out of trouble"
A Prisoner from a North West Prison

"This class is like oxygen to me and really helped me after coming off drugs"
A Prisoner from a North West Prison

"The lads on the wing really benefit from these sessions"
A Prisoner from a North West Prison

"Each click of the camera is a moment in time...an interaction and a memory...I like that"

Mick Steff | Photographer

Printed in Great Britain
by Amazon